MUSIC MINUS ONE TROMBONE

Standards for Trombone

3935

3935

MUSIC MINUS ONE TROMBONE

Standards for Trombone

CONTENTS

ISBN 1-59615-865-8

SOLO TROMBONE

Teach Me Tonight

Words and Music by
Sammy Cahn and Gene DePaul

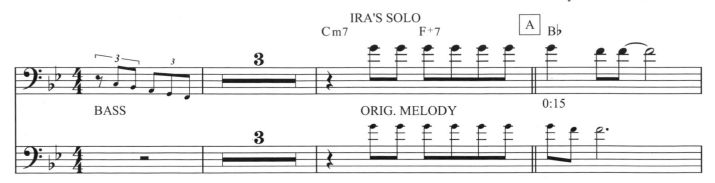

Did you say I've got a   lot to learn?

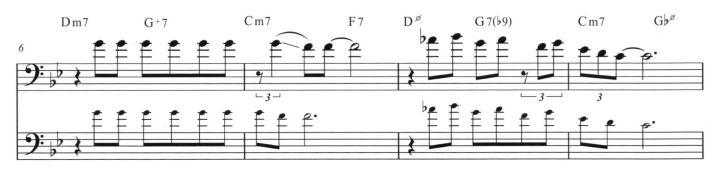

Well, don't think I'm try-ing   not to learn.   Since this is the per-fect spot to   learn,

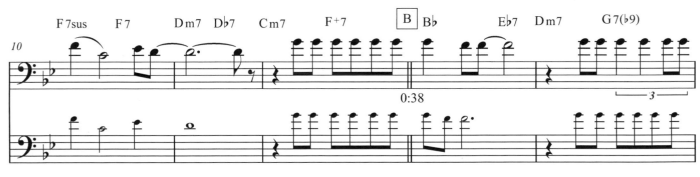

teach me   to - night.   Starting with the "A, B,   C" of it,   right down to the "X, Y,

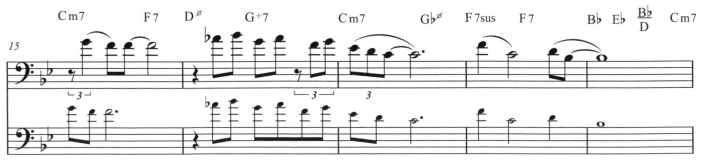

Z" of it.   Help me solve the mys-ter - y   of   it,   teach me   to - night.

The sky's a black - board high a - bove you. If a shoot - ing star goes

by, I'll use the star to write "I love you," a thou - sand times a - cross the

sky. One thing is - n't ver - y clear my love, Should the tea - cher stand so near my love?

Grad - u - a - tion's al - most here my love, teach me to - night. _____

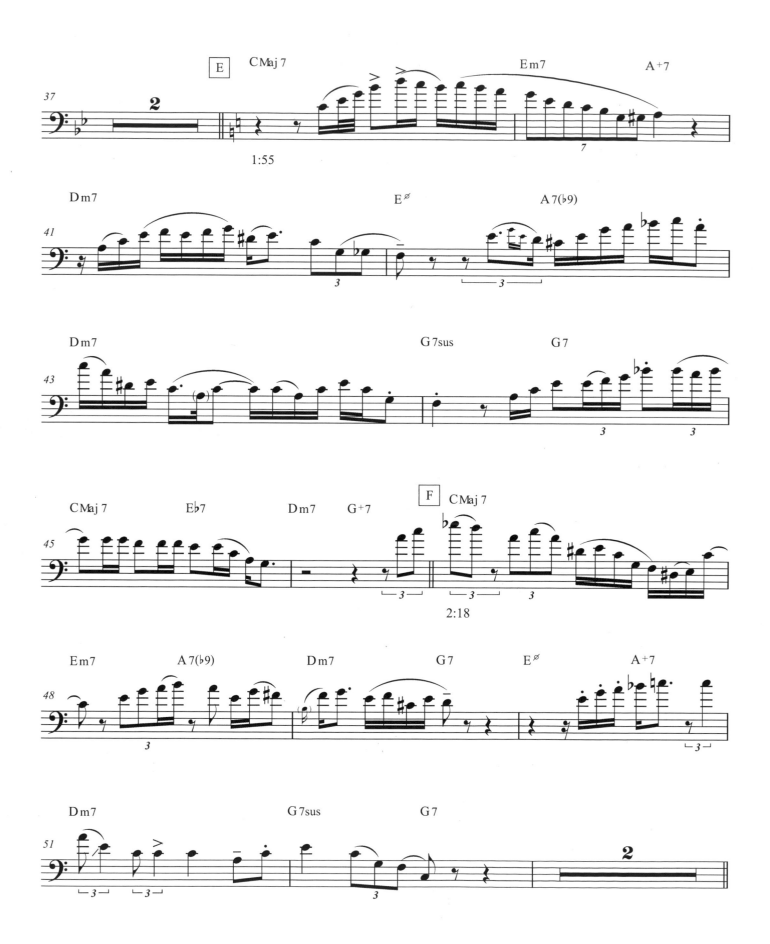

SOLO TROMBONE

Blue Bossa

Music by Kenny Dorham

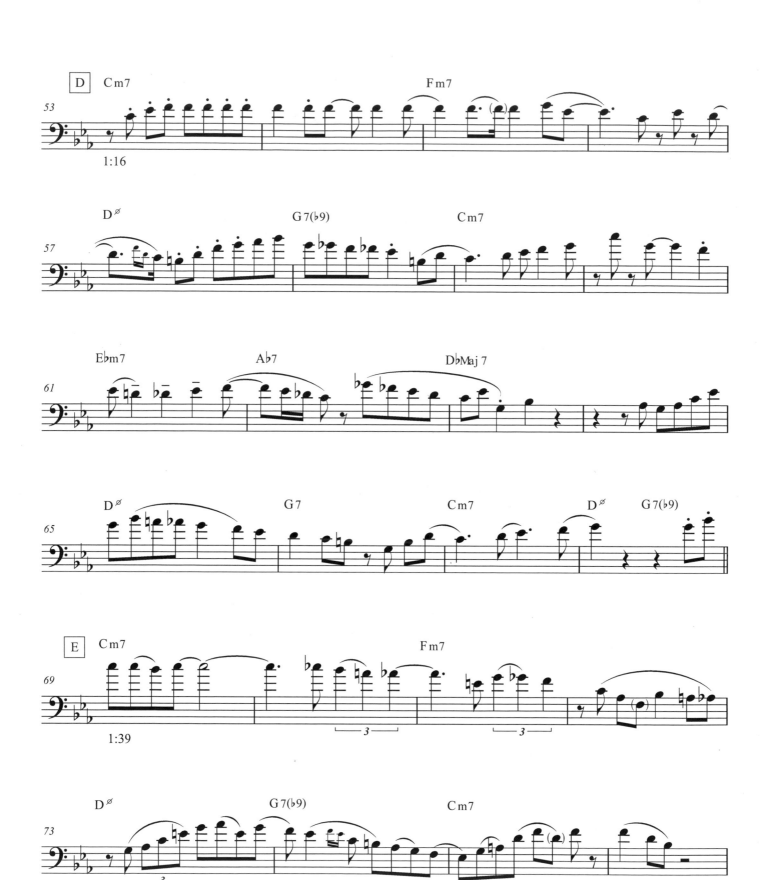

12

SOLO TROMBONE

Stardust

Hoagy Carmichael/
Mitchell Parish

SOLO TROMBONE

Lester Leaps In

Music by Lester Young

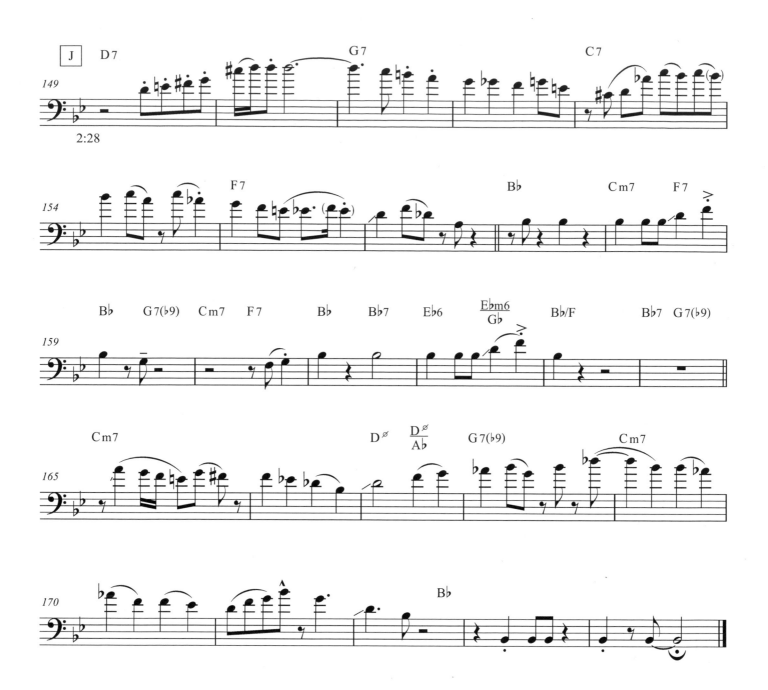

Music Minus One
DISTINGUISHED ACCOMPANIMENT EDITIONS

Trombone

Chamber Classics
Baroque Brass and Beyond: Quintets ....MMO CD 3904 $29.98
Classical Trombone Solos ....MMO CD 3909 $29.98
Music for Brass Ensemble...MMO CD 3905 $29.98
Sticks & Bones: Brass Quintets...MMO CD 3927 $29.98
STRAVINSKY L'Histoire du Soldat ....MMO CD 3908 $29.98

Inspirational Classics
Christmas Memories..MMO CDG 1203 $19.98

Instrumental Classics with Orchestra
Band Aids: Concert Band Favorites ....MMO CD 3930 $29.98
Popular Concert Favorites w/Orch ....MMO CD 3929 $29.98

Jazz, Standards and Big Band
2+2=5: A Study Odd Times ....MMO CD 2044 $19.98
Bacharach Revisited ....MMO CD 3974 $24.98
Back to Basics in the Style of the Basie Band...................................MMO CD 3985 $19.98
Big Band Ballads: Tenor or Bass Trombone ....MMO CD 3907 $19.98
From Dixie to Swing ....MMO CD 3926 $19.98
Isle of Orleans ....MMO CD 3933 $19.98
Jazz Standards w/Strings ....MMO CD 3910 $19.98
New Orleans Classics ....MMO CD 3934 $19.98
Northern Lights ....MMO CD 2004 $19.98
PCH Pacific Coast Horns, vol. 1: Longhorn Serenade...........................MMO CD 3975 $19.98
PCH Pacific Coast Horns, vol. 2:
  76 Trombones and other favs (Int-Adv) ....MMO CD 3976 $19.98
PCH Pacific Coast Horns, vol. 3: Where Trombone Reigns (Int-Adv) ....MMO CD 3977 $19.98
Play Ballads w/a Band...MMO CD 3972 $19.98
Standards for Trombone (Ira Lepus, trombone) ....MMO CD 3935 $24.98
Studio City..MMO CD 2024 $19.98
Swing with a Band ....MMO CD 3973 $19.98
Take One (minus Lead Trombone) ....MMO CD 2014 $19.98
Chicago-Style Jam Session..MMO CD 3921 $19.98
Adventures in N.Y. & Chicago Jazz ....MMO CD 3923 $19.98
Unsung Hero: Great Sinatra Standards ....MMO CD 3906 $19.98

Laureate Master Series Concert Solos
Beginning Solos, v. I (Brevig)..MMO CD 3911 $19.98
Beginning Solos, v. II (Friedman) ....MMO CD 3912 $19.98
Int. Solos, v. I (Brown)..MMO CD 3913 $19.98
Int. Solos, v. II (Friedman) ....MMO CD 3914 $19.98
Advanced Solos, v. I (Brown) ....MMO CD 3915 $19.98
Advanced Solos, v. II (Brevig) ....MMO CD 3916 $19.98
Advanced Solos, v. III (Brown) ....MMO CD 3917 $19.98
Advanced Solos, v. IV (Friedman) ....MMO CD 3918 $19.98
Advanced Solos, v. V (Brevig) ....MMO CD 3919 $19.98

Student Series
Classic Themes: 27 Easy Songs ....MMO CD 3932 $19.98
Easy Jazz Duets 2 Trombs/Rhythm Section.......................................MMO CD 3903 $19.98
Easy Solos: Student Level, v. I...MMO CD 3901 $19.98
Easy Solos: Student Level, v. II ....MMO CD 3902 $19.98
Teacher's Partner: Basic Studies ....MMO CD 3920 $19.98
Twelve Classic Jazz Standards ....MMO CD 7010 $19.98
Twelve More Classic Jazz Standards...MMO CD 7011 $19.98
World Favorites: 41 Easy Selections ....MMO CD 3931 $19.98

All Prices Subject To Change

SOLO TROMBONE

Black Orpheus

By Luiz Bonfa
and Antonio Carlos Jobim

MMO 3935

SOLO TROMBONE

Red Sails in the Sunset

Words and Music by
Jimmy Kennedy and Hugh Williams

MMO 3935

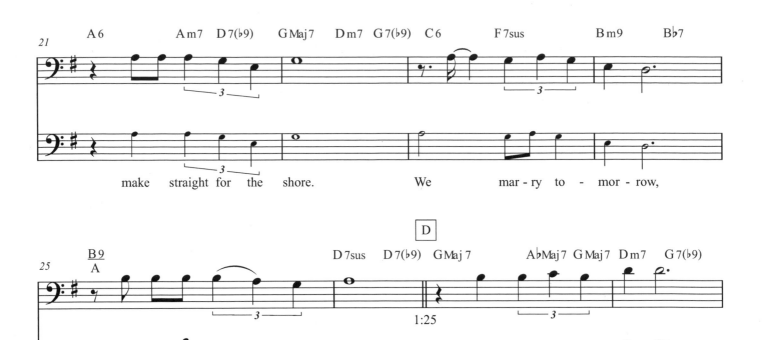

make straight for the shore. We mar - ry to - mor - row,

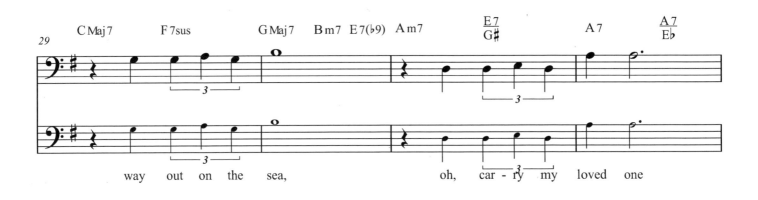

and he goes sail - ing no more.____ Red sails in the sun - set

way out on the sea, oh, car - ry my loved one

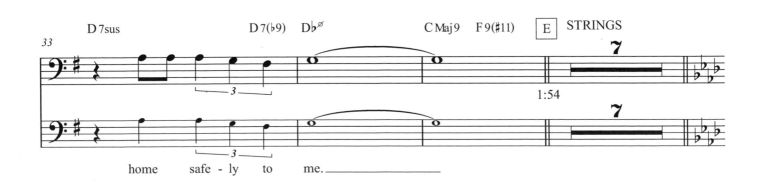

home safe - ly to me.____

2:16

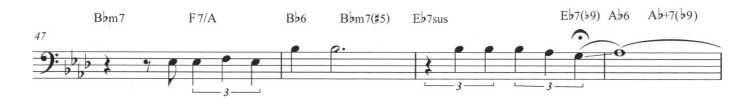

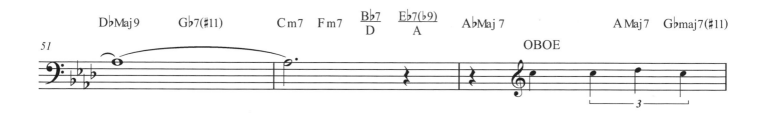

SOLO TROMBONE

Too Marvelous For Words

Words by Johnny Mercer
Music by Richard A. Whiting

SOLO TROMBONE

Samba de Orfeo
(Samba de Orphee)

Words by Antonio Maria and Andre Salvet
Music by Luiz Bonfá

MMO 3935

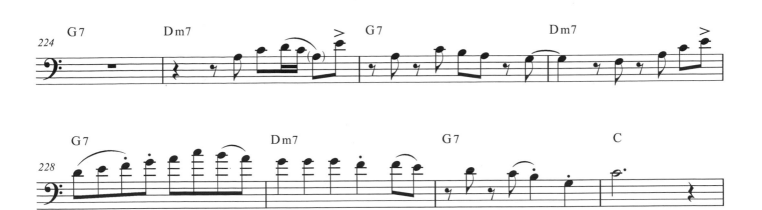

SOLO TROMBONE

My Foolish Heart

Words and Music by
Ned Washington and Victor Young

SOLO TROMBONE

When You're Smiling

Words and Music by Mark Fisher,
Joe Goodwin and Larry Shay

be hap - py a - gain! ___ Keep on smil - ing, 'cause when you're

smil - ing, the whole world smiles with you.

MUSIC MINUS ONE
50 Executive Boulevard
Elmsford, New York 10523-1325
800-669-7464 (US) • 914-592-1188 (International)

www.musicminusone.com
e-mail: info@musicminusone.com

MMO 3935

ISBN 1-59615-865-8